VANGUARD SERIES

EDITOR: MARTIN WINDROW

ALLIED
TANK DESTROYERS

Text by BRYAN PERRETT

Colour plates by MIKE CHAPPELL

OSPREY PUBLISHING LONDON

Published in 1979 by
Osprey Publishing Ltd
Member company of the George Philip Group
12–14 Long Acre, London WC2E 9LP
© Copyright 1979 Osprey Publishing Ltd

ISBN 0 85045 315 1

Filmset by BAS Printers Limited,
Over Wallop, Hampshire
Printed in Hong Kong

The author would like to thank Colonel Robert J. Icks
for his invaluable advice; also Mr Theodore H.
Aschman Jr and Mr Albert Baybutt. Thanks are also
due to Mr John J. Slonaker of the United States Army
Military History Institute and Brigadier R. J.
Lewendon of the Royal Artillery Institution for
permitting access to their records. Some of the
material on colour Plate G is taken from the published
researches of the Company of Military Historians,
USA. We are grateful to M. Daniel Ambrogi and John
Sandars for their assistance with Plates C, D and G.
Mike Chappell's cover painting depicts an M10 of
the HQ Company, 899th Tank Destroyer Bn., flying
the pennant of the 8th T.D. Group, against the
background of the Ludendorff railway bridge at
Remagen, March 1945. The insignia on the back
cover are the shoulder patch of the US Tank
Destroyer Forces, and the Royal Artillery cap badge
normally worn by British tank destroyer crews,
1943–45.

2pdr. portee and crew at range practice. In action as many of the crew as possible worked on the ground, as a direct hit would often dismount the gun, which would be thrown backwards, killing or injuring the men on the vehicle. (Imperial War Museum)

Prescience

In 1914 William Albert Murley joined the Royal Regiment of Artillery. He was commissioned the following year, and before the Great War had ended he had been awarded the Military Cross. Between the wars promotion for Regular officers was slow, but by 1939 he had reached the rank of major, having held a variety of appointments, including that of Permanent Staff Instructor to a Territorial regiment. He served throughout World War II and retired as a lieutenant-colonel in 1946. Ostensibly, his thirty-two years of service had followed the pattern of hundreds of his contemporaries; but there was a difference.

In 1923, while still a lieutenant, he gave a great deal of thought to the problems of anti-tank defence, and he set down his conclusions in an article which was printed the same year in the *Royal Artillery Journal*. He began by criticizing the British Army's current anti-tank gun, the 3.7in howitzer. He pointed out that it lacked the essential characteristic of an anti-tank weapon, all round traverse—the 3.7's traverse was limited to 40 degrees on the top carriage. The weapon had insufficient muzzle velocity; it lacked mobility over rough going; and it required the dumping of large quantities of ammunition beside the gun.

Next, he took issue with anti-tank tactics prescribed in the *Manual of Artillery Training*, which suggested that 'When engaging tanks with guns giving only a limited degree of traverse, a section [i.e. two guns] should be employed against each tank.' Murley commented that 'any method which necessitates the changing of a target from one gun to another is bound to be unsatisfactory, as there will nearly always be delay in getting the second gun to open fire at the proper moment, and unless both guns shoot exactly alike, which would be very doubtful, erratic shooting will result'.

The solution to these problems, he felt, lay in the adoption of the 6pdr. gun in place of the 3.7in howitzer, and he went on to describe how it could be done.

'(a) It should be possible to fix a central pivot mounting to a tank chassis, thus admitting all-round traverse. The recoil of the 6pdr. is short and the base plate to which the pedestal is bolted would

The Deacon, last of the portees. It was outranged even before it entered service. (RAC Tank Museum)

therefore have to be fairly thick in order to withstand the shock of the firing of the gun. As the gun will be mounted on a central pivot it will be possible to traverse it rapidly in any required direction. The target could therefore be engaged in a fraction of the time taken with the 3.7in howitzer, and when once on the target the layer could follow it anywhere by simply swinging the gun round. Also, the layer will have only the elevating wheel and firing handle to worry about, which will result in more rapid and accurate shooting. It may be necessary to fit a traversing handwheel, but if so, a quick release clamp should also be provided.

'(b) The fact of the 6pdr. being a gun and not a howitzer will enable greater muzzle velocity to be obtained. The extra muzzle velocity of the 6pdr. would compensate for the difference in weight of shell. The type of shell suggested for use with the 6pdr. is an armour-piercing with a delay action fuse. A 6pdr. is quite heavy enough to stop a tank.

'(c) The fact of the gun being mounted on a tank chassis would increase its mobility. *It is not suggested that the anti-tank gun should go out to meet the tank, but the fact of the gun being able to move quickly would permit a certain amount of manoeuvre, and the gun could therefore take up any previously selected position at a moment's notice. Under present conditions it would seem that a gun must take up a position and hope that a tank will appear, and if one should appear it may not be possible for the gun to engage it.* [Author's italics]

'(d) With the gun mounted on a tank chassis there should be no difficulty in arranging for the carrying of at least one hundred rounds of ammunition, so the difficulty of dumping ammunition will disappear. The ammunition could be placed in a kind of box on wheels running on a circular track, thus ensuring that it will always be close to the breech.

'The next point to consider is the protection of the detachment against rifle bullets and splinters. It should be a simple matter to provide a circular shield about ¼in or ½in thick. The shield would be bolted to the carriage, so that when the gun is moved the shield moves with it. The fact of the shield moving with the gun will permit of all-round traverse and will also afford protection of the detachment against fire from *any* direction.

'The engine could be driven from inside the shield, so that the driver would not be exposed to fire. Two Lewis guns could also be carried for use through movable [sliding] slots in case of emergency.'

Murley concluded his article by submitting with due deference that his suggestions were worth a trial; but in the political and national climate of the time, very similar to today's, there was not the slightest chance of their being accepted, although some years later the short-lived Birch Gun (an 18pdr. field piece on a Vickers Medium tank chassis) was produced.

The significance of Murley's article is that not only did it predict the layout of the typical World War II turreted tank destroyer, but also forecast the sort of tactics which would be employed. It would be too easy to suggest that Murley conceived the idea of the tank destroyer; very possibly other officers around the world were thinking along similar lines, although it would be many years before their thoughts turned to substance. In such circumstances one cannot help wondering what might have been the thoughts of the now middle-aged lieutenant-colonel in 1945, as the Allied armies swarmed across Europe using hundreds of the type of vehicle he had suggested building more than twenty years earlier.

In fact the British Army had entered World War II without any self-propelled artillery at all, whether field or anti-tank, and the lack of it was cruelly felt for several years. It was true that the guns had a new mobility due to the replacement of the old horse teams with motor traction units, but this had only been achieved after a struggle, which in some measure also contributed to the failure to develop self-propelled artillery.

Opposition to mechanization within the Royal Artillery was not simply a matter of bloody-minded anti-radicalism, an ultra-conservative rejection of the concept of total mobility as defined by the fashionable 'Armoured Idea'. Nor was it the product of sentimental affection for the 'hairies' which had always dragged the guns into action and which had always been the gunners' constant companions. Artillerymen are, after all, practical people, and it seemed to many that as long as some of the team were on their feet it would always be possible to attempt recovery of a gun from a difficult situation. Internal combustion engines, on the other hand, were subject to breakdown, and this could lead to the loss of a towed gun unless other vehicles were on hand to lend assistance; in the case of a self-propelled gun engine failure during a withdrawal would almost certainly lead to its loss, an idea abhorrent to a Regiment which had always fought to the muzzle and beyond as a matter of course. In the end it was the distances involved in mechanized operations that led to the demise of the horse teams—although, curiously, the majority of German field batteries outside armoured formations remained horse-drawn throughout the war.

On its own, the horse team versus internal combustion engine debate could not have delayed the introduction of self-propelled artillery into the British Army for long. The Birch Gun battery serving with the Experimental Armoured Force were enthusiastic about its rôle, for which they saw a great future. It was unfortunate that senior officers of the Royal Artillery and the then Royal Tank Corps got on extremely badly. The brilliant and irascible Colonel P. C. S. Hobart, RTC, later to command the famous 79th Armoured Division, for some reason could not tolerate Gunner officers and made no bones about it; he added fuel to the flames by speaking of self-propelled guns as 'Royal Tank Artillery'. To Woolwich this sounded rather like an attempted take-over, and the very cool response was that if the Royal Tank Corps wanted self-propelled guns to support its operations it should modify some of its tanks accordingly. This is simply the tip of the iceberg, and the whole story is an excellent example of British military tribalism at its worst, the net result being the waste of the best part of a decade during which research and development could profitably have been pursued. Nor should it be forgotten that for most of the inter-

75mm Gun Motor Carriage M3, with front and side-door screens raised. (RAC Tank Museum)

war period the Army as a whole was forced to work within stringent financial limits, and no funds could be spared for projects upon which there was a lack of common agreement on policy and which did not seemingly bear the stamp of immediacy.

In 1973 the editor of the *Royal Artillery Journal*, looking for items of interest from fifty years earlier, came across William Murley's article, and had it reprinted with the comment that the young author had shown considerable prescience. By then the big gun tank destroyer had become a battlefield memory for as long after the event as it had been Murley's vision before it; but in the few years of its active life it had had a most interesting and unusual career.

The Concept

The dramatic success of the German *blitzkrieg* technique in Poland, France, the Balkans and the Western Desert illustrated beyond any reasonable doubt that a defensive cordon of towed anti-tank guns was not the answer to a massed tank attack, particularly if the tanks were closely supported by aircraft and infantry. Once the cordon had been ruptured the tanks moved too quickly for further defensive fronts to be constructed across their path, and the containment of such breakthroughs seemed to present insuperable difficulties for armies equipped with conventional artillery.

In the still neutral United States the problem was studied carefully at the highest levels. Within the United States Army, as within every army of the period, there had been a debate as to whether the best defence against the tank was the anti-tank gun or another tank. Events abroad seemed to indicate that the anti-tank gun had failed in its primary mission; but the tank represented an expensive solution, and in any event the Chief of the Armored Force did not wish his vehicles to be employed in a defensive rôle, as the nature and training of his arm was specifically designed for offensive operations.

On the other hand, the anti-tank gun was potentially a more powerful weapon than that carried by the majority of contemporary tanks, and if it could be given a self-propelled mobility it could be deployed and re-deployed rapidly to deal with any developing crisis, which the towed gun could not.

M3 with armoured screens lowered. (US Army)

On 14 May 1941 General George C. Marshall, Chief of Staff United States Army, issued a directive for the establishment of an organization, armed with an *offensive* weapon, whose function would be defence against armoured forces. In his directive Marshall emphasized that this 'was a problem beyond the capabilities of any one arm and probably required the organization and use of a special force of combined arms, capable of rapid movement, interception and active rather than passive defence tactics'[1]

The following day Lt.-Col. Andrew D. Bruce was detailed to set up a planning branch for the new organization, designed to look into the questions of equipment, training and administration. By the end of November the planning phase had been completed, and Bruce was appointed to command the new Tank Destroyer Tactical and Firing Center at its temporary headquarters at Fort George G. Meade, Maryland. In accordance with the new concept of aggressive defence, existing anti-tank battalions were re-designated Tank Destroyer battalions the following month.

The task facing Bruce was enormous. He had to build a central administrative organization for the rapidly expanding Tank Destroyer Force, and at the same time formulate doctrine, organize training, superintend weapons development, and prepare tables of organization. With very limited resources he was founding what amounted to a new arm of service, starting from scratch.

The basic thinking behind the new arm was simple. Mobile tank destroyers in large numbers

[1] *The Tank Destoyer History*. Study No. 29, Historical Section, Army Ground Forces.

would be deployed rapidly in the path and on the flanks of any enemy mass tank attack, where they would destroy their opponents by direct gunfire. In Bruce's own words, 'Panther-like, we seek *information* of enemy tanks and of suitable firing positions; panther-like, we strike and destroy by *gunfire* from favourable positions. This does not mean that we seek out tanks with guns, nor chase them, nor pursue them, nor charge them.'[1] In the years that followed, this was emphasized time and again in training circulars: 'The primary mission of

tank destroyer units is the destruction of hostile tanks by [the direct] fire of a superior mass of guns.'[2] The choice of a panther head for a badge and a motto of *Seek, Strike and Destroy* were constant reminders of the new methods.

Belligerent mottoes are not usually taken too seriously by the men who actually do the fighting.

[1] *Ibid.*

[2] Training Circulars 88 and 125, June and November 1943.

The normal recoil of the M1897-A4 75mm gun was 43in. This photograph illustrates the sharply tapered construction of the barrel and the method of its carriage in the recoil slides. (RAC Tank Museum)

Following the arrival of the first M10s in North Africa, a number of M3s were handed over to the French Army, which imposed its own mottled sand colour scheme. (ECP Armées)

In this case occasional over-usage by instructors sometimes led to irreverent yells of 'Shag Ass!' a coarse expression which might be translated as 'It sounds unpleasant—I'm not stopping to find out!' In spite of this the TD soldier was proud of his trade, and reckoned he was a better all-round soldier than anyone else in the Army.

The basic unit was the battalion, of which initially there were three types, as follows:

Heavy, Self-Propelled: Headquarters Company and three gun companies with a total of twenty-four 3in or 75mm anti-tank guns, twelve M6 37mm anti-tank guns and eighteen 37mm anti-aircraft guns, all self-propelled. A Reconnaissance Company equipped with M3 halftracks (later M8 armoured cars) was added to this establishment, performing the invaluable service of route finding and selection of fire positions for the battalion. The 37mm anti-aircraft guns were later replaced by dual mount .50 cal. machine guns in M3 halftracks, and the M6 light tank destroyers replaced by the heavier weapons.

Light, Self-Propelled: Similar establishment to Heavy Battalion, but equipped with thirty-six M6 37mm anti-tank guns and eighteen dual mount .50 cal. anti-aircraft machine guns, all self-propelled. The light tank destroyer was soon seen to fall below battlefield requirements, and units so equipped were converted to the Heavy rôle.

Light, Towed: Similar establishment to Light SP battalion, and equipped with thirty-six towed 37mm anti-tank guns and eighteen dual mount .50 cal. anti-aircraft machine guns, self-propelled. The

TDF did not dispense with towed anti-tank guns altogether, and at one phase there was even an increase in the proportion of towed guns. The 37mm was replaced by the 3in anti-tank gun M1.

The heavy anti-aircraft element within each battalion was a clear indication that the dive-bombing attacks which had disrupted the British and French static anti-tank gun cordons would have less success against the new American formations. In the event, the twin (and later, quadruple) .50 mounting was used extensively against ground targets as well, with such murderously successful results that it earned itself the title of 'the meat grinder'.

As already mentioned, tank destroyers were designed to operate *en masse* and the next step up the formation ladder from battalion was the Tank Destroyer Group, consisting of a group Headquarters and HQ Company, plus three TD battalions. The largest formation of all was the Tank Destroyer Brigade, which included a Headquarters and two TD Groups. As originally conceived one TD Brigade would support each corps, and two each army; in fact only two such brigades were raised and of these only one, the 1st, saw active service.

The Tank Destroyer Tactical and Firing Center began moving from Fort Meade to a new permanent station named Camp Hood at Killeen, Texas, in the middle of January 1942. Once established, the Tank Destroyer Center was able to concentrate on the training of individuals and units. The men came from the cavalry, the artillery

M3 in British service, firing in the supplementary artillery rôle. Maximum elevation obtainable was +29 degrees. (RAC Tank Museum)

and the infantry; the first task was to establish a common standard of training, including the use of small arms and explosives, after which they learned their basic TD crew trade. Training of entire battalions took about three months, including five weeks' gunnery and range practice, six weeks' tactics, and one week's battle conditioning.[1] In addition to training new battalions, the TD Center established its own Officer Candidate School and a Replacement Training Center, designed to keep battalions in the field at full strength. A total of 5,187 officers and 17,062 enlisted men qualified on courses conducted by the TD School, while 42,000 enlisted men passed through the Replacement Training Center and 5,299 2nd lieutenants graduated from the Officer Candidate School. The unit

M10s in Tunisia. The complete absence of stowage suggests that the vehicles are in transit to join their battalions; the undamaged condition of the sandshields seems to support this view. Note tank crash-helmets, later generally replaced for crews of open vehicles by steel helmets. (Imp. War Mus.)

training record was equally impressive, including two Brigade and twenty-four Group Headquarters, and 100 battalions. In the equipment field the Tank Destroyer Board had developed the M18 Tank Destroyer and evaluated the bazooka on behalf of the Army.[2]

Because of his vastly increased responsibilities, Lieutenant-Colonel Bruce was promoted to Brigadier-General in February 1942 and to Major-General in September of that year. He handed over command of the Tank Destroyer Center to Major-General Orlando C. Ward on 25 May 1943. His achievement should not be seen as simply a brilliant piece of administration; prior to the establishment of the TDF the US Army had serious doubts that it

---

[1]The Tank Destroyer Center established something of a first in its battle conditioning methods, in that advancing troops were fired on from the front with live ammunition, instead of from the flanks; this was frightening, realistic and effective.

[2]*The Tank Destroyer History.*

could meet the Panzer Divisions on equal terms—those doubts no longer existed.

General Ward had commanded 1st Armored Division in North Africa and had seen the new tank destroyer battalions in action. He was able to comment on what was good battle practice and what was not, and instituted a series of 'battle plays' to emphasize the lessons, as well as having signs placed around the ranges illustrating good and bad combat firing positions. Under Ward the Tank Destroyer Center reached its maximum expansion, and at one time there were more guns at Camp Hood than the total of all the divisional artillery pieces possessed by the American Expeditionary Force in World War I.

Thereafter, the importance of the arm declined and the TD Center contracted rapidly towards its eventual inactivation. There were several reasons for this. First, by the autumn of 1943 the US Army had achieved the strength required to attain its strategic objectives. Secondly, the German mass

tank attack was no longer the threat it had been in 1940 to 1941. Thirdly, tanks were inevitably fighting tanks on the battlefield, regardless of doctrine. Finally, such progress had been made in tank design that tanks were now capable of carrying guns of greater range and killing-power than those carried by the tank destroyers; in fact, there was some danger of the hunters becoming the hunted.

The Weapons:

General Bruce had been quite clear from the outset about the sort of weapon he was looking for. 'What we are after is a fast-moving vehicle, armed with a weapon with a powerful punch which can be easily and quickly fired, and in the last analysis we would like to get armoured protection against small arms fire so that this weapon cannot be put out of action by a machine gun.'[1] He wanted 'a cruiser, not a battleship', and he favoured the employment of the Christie suspension, which provided the best basis for high speed cross-country movement.

A scene in the Anzio beachhead on 3 May 1944. The M10 is standing by in the counter-attack rôle, and its suspension has been protected against ground strafing by enemy aircraft; otherwise, its crew seem to be very poor housekeepers, even allowing for the conditions of static war! (Imp. War Mus.)

[1] *Ibid.*

75mm Gun Motor Carriage M3

Pending the appearance of such a vehicle, Bruce had to make do with whatever was available. There were several hundred old 75mm guns on hand, and Bruce learned from a French ordnance designer that this type of weapon had been mounted successfully on a 5-ton truck. It was decided that the American stock should be fitted to the M3 halftrack armoured personnel carrier, and Major Robert J. Icks was assigned to carry out the Ordnance Department's request for the gun and part of its field carriage to be mounted in the vehicle and test fired. Having completed this task at the Aberdeen Proving Ground, Icks delivered the vehicle to Fort Meade, where it underwent further tests and modifications before being sent to the Autocar Company of Ardmore, Pennsylvania, for the production run.

A total of 2,202 vehicles were converted, of which all but 842 were re-converted later to APCs. After the M18 entered service the M3 became a limited standard (i.e. second line) vehicle, but it served on in the British Army in the heavy troops of armoured car and divisional recce regiments. In general, the vehicles were popular with their crews and did their work well:

'They weighed ten tons and were equipped with a 75mm M1897-A4 gun. The normal rate of fire was six rounds per minute, but 26–28 rounds per minute was possible with a well-trained crew. The tube and breech of this gun weighed 1,035 pounds and the barrel had a uniform right-hand twist with 24 lands and grooves. Total traverse of the piece was 39 degrees, 20 right and 19 left. Consequently when we pulled into position, the wheels of the halftrack were cramped hard to the right. To gain more traverse to the left, the vehicle was backed up—more to the right, you pulled ahead. Elevation was from minus 10 degrees to plus 29. When firing, the vehicle was always left in neutral gear with the engine running. Normal recoil of the piece was 43in, and on more than one occasion the loader was knocked flat. On our vehicles we used an M33 fixed sight—a simple but effective sight with lead and range markings.'[1]

37mm Gun Motor Carriage M6

There were numerous designs contending for

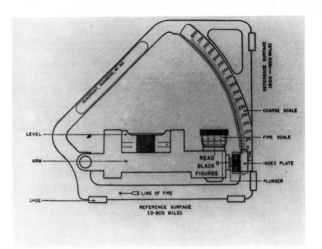

The gunner's quadrant, which, mounted on the breech block and used in conjunction with the traverse indication, permitted tank destroyers to engage in indirect firing.

standardization as the TDF's light tank destroyer—so many, in fact, that there was a saying that the Army had mounted a gun 'on anything and everything from a roller skate up'. A total of nineteen vehicles in the light class were developed, nine mounting the 37mm gun, seven a 40mm gun, and three a 57mm gun. Of these the 37mm mounted on a ¾-ton truck was standardized as the GMC M6, and 3,117 were produced. In layout the M6 followed that of the British 2pdr. *portees* already fighting in the Western Desert, and indeed the two guns had a very similar performance. The light class of tank destroyer was intended as an expedient, volume production measure pending the appearance of larger vehicles, but some did serve in North Africa.

3in Gun Motor Carriage M10

Meanwhile the General Motors Corporation and the Ford Motor Company were producing a tank destroyer based on the M4A2 medium tank chassis. In accordance with the Tank Destroyer Board's specification it had an angled hull and an open-topped turret, capable of all-round traverse, mounting a 3in high-velocity gun.

When General Bruce examined the vehicle at the Aberdeen Proving Ground on 2 May 1942 he was against its being accepted as a standard weapon system. At thirty tons he felt it was too heavy; with a top speed of 30mph he felt it was too slow. Nonetheless it was accepted as standard, and became the best-known of all the US Army's tank destroyers. It was constructed in two versions, the

[1]Theodore H. Aschman Jr, 814th Tank Destroyer Battalion.

Elements of the American advance guard in Rome, 4 June 1944.
Details of the close-defence .50 cal. mounting and stowage of
'ready' ammunition are clearly visible on the M10 in the
foreground. Behind is an M4 medium tank and one of the
unpopular M8 armoured cars. (Imp. War Mus.)

M10 and the M10A1, of which the former was
more popular with its crews:

'The M10 motor carriage, powered by two diesel
engines, proved to be a very good self-propelled
mount. The main advantages were: (1) the
flexibility of the two motors, which made it possible
to move after one had been knocked out or failed in
operation; (2) the power of the diesel motors at low
speed; (3) the increased range per gallon of fuel;
(4) the ease of motor maintenance of the diesel
engine.

'The M10A1 motor carriage, powered by a
500hp Ford tank gasoline engine, also proved to be
a very sturdy and well-designed gun mount. The
units that were equipped with both the M10 and
M10A1 felt that the latter had a little less power
than the M10, that its one engine made it less
flexible, and that the gasoline engine was a little
harder to maintain and would not stand the rough

going as well as the diesel engines.'[1]

Over 6,700 M10s were built, and as well as being the TDF's primary weapon, the vehicle saw active service with the British, French and Russian armies.

90mm Gun Motor Carriage M36

The appearance in early 1943 of larger, better-armoured German tanks meant that the TDF needed a gun capable of greater penetration than the 3in carried by the M10, and the weapon chosen was a 90mm high-velocity AA gun. The basic M10 turret could not house this, so a new turret was designed and fitted to the M10 chassis, the new vehicle being accepted as standard and designated M36 in June 1944.

[1]*Study of Organisation, Equipment and Tactical Employment of Tank Destroyer Units*; General Board, US Forces, European Theatre, Study No. 60.

The 90mm gun was the most powerful carried by unmodified US tank destroyers. It could penetrate six inches of armour at 1,000 yards; at the same range it could penetrate five feet of reinforced concrete, using only two rounds as opposed to ten of 3in. Other improvements upon the M10 were thicker armour and the addition of a power traverse, although the rate of fire was slower because of the larger ammunition.

The M36 GMC proved to be an acceptable answer to the Tiger and total of 1,722 were built, including 500 converted M10A1s.

Near Isola del Piano, an M10 of 93rd Anti-Tank Regiment RA overtakes 5th Battalion, Sherwood Foresters. When moving into the line, tank destroyers often carried ammunition and consolidation stores for the infantry. The vehicle crew's packs are attached to an additional stowage rail which has been welded across the glacis plate. (Imp. War Mus.)

76mm Gun Motor Carriage M18

Unlike the M3, M10 and M36, the M18 was not a modification of existing equipment but had been designed 'from the ground up' as a purpose-built tank destroyer and came closest to the original concept of General Bruce and the Tank Destroyer Board (who, it will be recalled, had always sought high speed, hitting power and limited protection against small arms).

While the early preference for a Christie-type suspension had given way to a torsion bar system, the M18 barely topped 19 tons at combat weight and was driven by a 400hp engine, a power to weight ratio that made it the fastest tracked AFV of World War II and earned it the name of 'Hellcat'.

As originally planned, the M18 would have mounted a 75mm gun, but in September 1942 the Ordnance Department called Bruce's attention to a new 76mm gun which had been developed for the later models of the M4 medium tank series. 'This gun embodied the same physical characteristics as the 75mm, had the same breechblock, recoil and similar design of tube. Through a longer tube and the use of a larger cartridge case, a much higher muzzle velocity and a greater striking power were attained than with the 75mm gun, and that without an appreciable increase in weight. The 76mm gun was in reality a 76.2mm calibre weapon, equivalent to the 3in but much lighter in weight. It had the additional advantage over the 75mm of using the same projective [sic] as the 3in.'[1]

The M18 began entering service in the autumn of 1943, and was an immediate success. It 'proved to be an ideal *light* destroyer and was highly praised by the using troops. Into the design of this destroyer were built maintenance aids which proved of great value in combat. Two such aids were (1) the extension track for replacing engines, and (2) the removable frontal plate which made it possible to change the transmission in less than one hour. In a very large per cent of its employment in this theatre, its road speed of 60mph and its great cross-country speed were never needed. However, its flotation did prove to be a great advantage during the winter operations.'[2]

The Buick Division of General Motors manufactured a total of 2,507 M18s between July 1943 and October 1944. A turretless version, known as the Armored Utility M39, was employed as an APC, an ammunition carrier with a payload of 263 rounds, and as a prime mover for the towed 3in anti-tank guns M1 and M6.

M8 Light Armored Car and M20 Armored Utility Vehicle

'These vehicles were not popular with the tank destroyer units. The common complaints were: lack of power in the higher range of speeds; lack of flotation; lack of sufficient armour and armament; the open turret of the M8 and the open-top construction of the M20; the position of the driver and commander directly over the front wheels caused casualties whenever a mine was hit; the lack of sufficient operating room for the crew in the M20; and the vulnerability of the radiator to small arms fire. Maintenance was not difficult, but it was a major operation to get to the motor for even the first echelon check.'[3] The M20 was a command version of the M8, and was intended to carry a crew of six, plus two radios. It was also used as an APC and as a cargo carrier.

US Tank Destroyers in Combat

The Philippines, 1941–42

In December 1941 fifty 75mm M3 halftracks were hastily despatched to Luzon to bolster the island's defences. Details of their use is fragmentary, and one source indicates that 'they were used effectively as self-propelled artillery'. The majority were sent to the south of the island, but several were attached to the Provisional Tank Group which was contesting the principal Japanese axis of advance, from Lingayen Gulf south to Manila. The Japanese were using tanks on this axis, and quite heavy armoured engagements took place at Moncada and Baliuag. On the basis of the evidence available it seems very probable that the TDF's first victims were Type 89 and Type 97 medium tanks and Type 94 tankettes of the Japanese 7th Tank Regiment. The M3s were lost in the subsequent fighting and general surrender.

[1] *Tank Destroyer History*. In spite of this the two rounds were *not* interchangeable.
[2] Study No. 60.
[3] *Ibid*.

North Africa, 1942–43

The next vehicles to find themselves in the M3's gunsights were obsolete French tanks, and belonged to armoured units which briefly opposed the Allied landings in North Africa. A typical example was the action fought by 3rd Platoon, Company 'B', 701st Tank Destroyer Battalion at St Lucien, south of Oran, on 9 November 1942. The 3rd Platoon was supporting a light tank company,

Even weary infantry coming out of the line could not fail to comment on a sight such as this. The vehicle commander's explanation must have provided some interesting listening! Just visible on the front top decking of the turret is a British air recognition roundel. (Imp. War Mus.)

and began the engagement by knocking out two tanks at a range in excess of 2,000 yards, a range well beyond the capability of any tank on either side. The remaining twelve French vehicles were also disposed of without loss.

In British service the M10 was known as the Wolverine. This V Corps vehicle is seen being guided across the River Savio on 24 October 1944, using a causeway of Churchill ARKs. A 'dead' Panther lies beyond. The crew are clearly experienced at looking after themselves, as can be seen by the neat, secure stowage, the 'acquired' oversize funnel (an invaluable aid during replenishment), bivouac stakes and bucket. (Imp. War Mus.)

It was a small but optimistic beginning; but thereafter tank destroyer battalions in North Africa found themselves shamefully misused by senior commanders who did not properly understand their function. To quote Theodore Aschman, a former officer of 814th Tank Destroyer Battalion:

'The TDs were a sort of maverick. Regimental and divisional commanders looked upon us as a sort of makeshift organization and an expendable one at that. Often we were used as an attacking point and preceded the tanks—sort of a sacrificial lamb. We were (at least our battalion) never permanently assigned to any division. . . . We were always on the move, travelling from 200 to 300 miles during the night to be on hand for an engagement during the pre-dawn of the next day, after which we would pack up and move another one hundred or so miles. I made a dozen or so such trips across the top of Africa. On occasions, we would act like artillery and set up emplacements and lay in wait for ground troops. On other occasions we acted as infantry. To me it seemed that we did everything that no one else wanted to do. However, our *esprit de corps* was high, and I am sure that left to their own devices, the TDs would have done better the job for which they were organized. Patton, in his misguided wisdom, used them ineffectively, to the point that he placed them in tactical engagements for which they were not intended, in that he used them as tanks. My outfit was all but wiped out because of this, as was the 601st.'

In mid-February 1942 the Germans launched a massive armoured attack on the US II Corps. After penetration had been achieved, the plan called for

Front and rear views of 17pdr. SP anti-tank gun Archer. (Imp. War Mus.)

the panzer divisions to seize Kasserine Pass and then swing north-west, so isolating all 1st Allied Army's troops in southern Tunisia. It was a textbook situation which called for the deployment *en masse* of tank destroyer battalions. Unfortunately, the Americans responded with an armoured counter-attack of their own, which the Germans were expecting and with which they dealt severely. Such tank destroyers as were involved were employed in 'penny packets'.

By the evening of 14 February the US 1st Armored Division's Combat Command 'A' had been cut off on two hills east of Sidi Bou Zid. The following day a relief operation was mounted by the tanks of CCB, accompanied by Company 'B', 701st Tank Destroyer Battalion. The advance was made in open order, and the action is described from the TD's viewpoint:

'Our attack was launched about 1400hrs on the 15th from an assembly point some ten miles west of Sidi Bou Zid. The tanks of 2nd Battalion, 1st Armored Regiment were preceded by a light screen of reconnaissance. Our 3rd Platoon was to protect the right flank, the 2nd Platoon to support the centre and be ready to protect the left flank, and the 1st Platoon was to guard the rear and be ready to move to either flank. The artillery and infantry moved along with the rear elements.

'The enemy had had many hours' warning of our approach and had placed many 88s in position in and about Sidi Bou Zid. As our tanks drew close, two or three 88s would commence firing. Then as our tanks would concentrate on these and move in closer, having apparently silenced them, other 88s would open up. Tanks in the open were at a great disadvantage. After the battle had progressed for some time, enemy tanks moving from Faid menaced the right flank of our force. After the 3rd Platoon had moved out to meet this attack, other enemy tanks, proceeding from Lassouda, menaced the left flank. The reserve tank company was in the best position to meet this threat, but it set out in a mistaken direction. As our 2nd and 3rd Platoons (the latter had been called back from its mission to the right flank) were attempting to deal with the last threat a third enemy tank column closed in from the south. Our forces were being fired on from four directions. All that were not too far advanced beat a hasty retreat, or rather rout, our company abandoning one 37mm gun and one jeep. Only seven out of fifty-four medium tanks of the 2nd Battalion escaped from this well-conceived and perfectly executed trap.'[1] It took several days' hard fighting before the German threat was eventually contained.

Meanwhile, M10s were beginning to arrive in North Africa, and several battalions handed over their M3s to the under-equipped French, now firmly committed to the Allied cause. On 23 March an M10 battalion, the 899th, ahead of which lay a most distinguished combat record, showed what could be done. The day began badly when a spoiling attack by 10th Panzer Division overran the M3s of 601st TD Battalion near El Guettar after a night approach march. The panzers were then stalled by a minefield covered by the 899th's 'B' Company, which had moved hurriedly into position. Under the command of Lieutenant Gerald G. Coady, the M10s engaged in a six-hour fire fight across the minefield against the hull-down tanks, destroying ten PzKpfw IVs, damaging three more and knocking out two anti-tank guns, in exchange for five damaged TDs.

Meanwhile, 'C' Company had moved into position along a ridge from which 'it was possible to watch all the proceedings, just like one would watch an opera from a balcony seat'. After an air attack, the German infantry began to advance but walked into the American artillery's defensive barrage, and two PzKpfw IVs which ventured out in support were picked off at once by 'C' Company, as were a brace of APCs. 10th Panzer Division retired during the night, and it was with justifiable pride that the 899th's historian was able to write, 'This was the first time an American unit had stopped a German armoured attack'.[2]

On 7 April, while attached to Benson Force, the 899th became the first American unit to make contact with the left flank of the advancing British 8th Army.

In spite of its many frustrations, the North

314 Battery, 105 AT Regt. RA, on parade with their Archers shortly after the conclusion of hostilities.

African campaign vindicated the concept of the mobile tank destroyer. On the other hand, many senior American officers had been impressed by the British system of interlocked artillery and static in-depth anti-tank defence which had provided Rommel with such a signal defeat at Medenine. As a result of their reports the TDF was instructed in December 1943 that its establishment henceforth would be fifty per cent self-propelled and fifty per cent towed battalions, and some twenty self-propelled units were converted to the latter rôle.[3]

Italy

The Italian landscape did not permit the deployment of large armoured formations, and TD battalions serving in this theatre were largely confined to what was termed their Secondary Mission, that is providing direct and indirect fire in the rôle of supplementary artillery, supporting infantry operations, acting in the counter-attack rôle, and opportunity shooting. In this American practice varied little from British, and further details can be found in the British section of the book.

France and Germany

No sooner had the initial Normandy landings been completed than it became obvious that the towed anti-tank gun was entirely unsuitable for the *bocage*.

[1] *North African Campaign Diary*, 'B' Company, 701st TD Bn. and 2nd Plt Rcn Company, 701st TD Bn.
[2] *TD—A Brief History of the 899th Tank Destroyer Battalion.*
[3] Study No. 60.

It was unable to fire over the hedge-topped banks, could cover only a limited arc, was difficult to emplace and was easily lost if the local infantry were forced to give ground. In consequence, there was an immediate clamour for self-propelled TDs. Simultaneously, the appearance of well-armed and heavily armoured tanks and tank hunters on the German side led to a request that the M10s should be replaced by M36s.

By September 1944 a new policy had begun to take shape. Only twelve of the fifty-two battalions in the theatre would remain towed; twenty battalions would be equipped with the M36, and the remainder with the M10 or M18 as available. Later losses during the Ardennes campaign spelled the doom of the towed gun, and by the end of hostilities all towed units had either been converted or were scheduled to convert to the SP rôle.[1]

By now there was a general acceptance that TD commanders, as the experts in direct shooting, should be permitted to execute assigned missions in accordance with their training and without interference from above. As well as carrying out their Primary Mission of destroying enemy armour, TDs also acted extensively as assault guns for infantry formations, destroying pillboxes, bunkers and other fortifications, and as supplementary artillery. Unfortunately their very popularity tended to work against the rôle for which they had been designed, for once a formation had acquired the support of a TD company it was most reluctant to relinquish it. This meant that the TD battalion commander could be left without a single platoon under his

Although the two vehicles were carried on similar suspensions, the M36 (right) can easily be distinguished from the M10 (left) by its larger gun and distinctive turret. (Imp. War Mus.)

immediate command, with the result that it was not always possible to co-ordinate a mobile anti-tank defence in an emergency.

On the other hand, local actions by TD companies could prevent a most serious situation developing. At 0200hrs on 11 July 1944 the *Panzer Lehr* Division launched a thrust at Isigny, determined to cut the American beachhead in two. The German attack was canalized by marshes on either flank, and directly in its path lay the 899th Tank Destroyer Battalion, the victors of El Guettar, with Companies 'A' and 'C' supporting respectively the 39th and 47th Infantry Regiments. In a desperate close-quarter night action the TDs halted the enemy's advance, 'A' Company destroying six Panthers, one PzKpfw IV and an assault gun, while 'C' Company accounted for a further six Panthers. Shortly after dawn the Germans' exploitation force was discovered a mile down the road and destroyed by bombing. Both companies received almost identical Presidential Citations for this action, and that of 'A' Company is quoted below.

'Company 'A', 899th Tank Destroyer Battalion

[1] 610 Tank Destroyer Battalion actually went through the whole range of TD equipment. In January 1943 it was equipped with M3s, and converted to M10s in July of that year. During the following winter it was converted to the towed rôle, and fought its way across France with towed guns. In September 1944 the battalion was reassigned as a self-propelled unit and equipped with M36s. When the war ended it was in process of exchanging these for M18s.

is cited for outstanding performance of duty in action on 11 July 1944, near St Jean de Daye, France. Company 'A' was supporting 39th Infantry in a defense rôle near St Jean de Daye. At 0200hrs on the morning of 11 July 1944 the enemy launched a combined armored and infantry attack in this sector. Two columns of heavy tanks with supporting infantry smashed through and penetrated to the rear of this position in an attempt to capture St Jean de Daye and to sever the Allied beachhead. Outgunned and outnumbered, and despite the fact that the enemy infantry threatened to overrun their tank destroyers, the men of Company 'A' fearlessly remained in position and fired on enemy tanks wherever discernible in the darkness, fully realizing that the flash of each round would draw not only artillery and tank fire but also small arms fire as well. As daylight appeared, Company 'A', aware that their 3in guns could not penetrate the heavy frontal armor of the Panther tanks, boldly manoeuvred their tank destroyers under close enemy observation to flanking positions where effective fire was placed on the enemy tanks. Forced to fight at extremely close quarters and at point-blank ranges, the officers and men of Company 'A' gallantly and courageously repelled numerous attempts of the enemy to seize these positions. So effective was their fire that the enemy was forced to withdraw their remaining tanks from the action, leaving the infantry in small isolated pockets which were quickly overcome by our forces. The individual courage, valor, and tenacity displayed by the personnel of Company 'A' in the face of superior odds were in keeping with the highest traditions of the Armed Forces and are worthy of high praise.

By command of Major-General Craig:
William C. Westmoreland,
Colonel, G.S.C., Chief of Staff.'

The identity of the signatory will be of interest to students of more recent military history.

The higher TD formation headquarters were not used extensively. The 1st Tank Destroyer Brigade HQ commanded Third Army's Task Force 'A', whose mission was to assist in clearing the Brittany Peninsula. Task Force 'A' consisted of 2nd and 15th Cavalry Groups, 6th TD Group plus 705th TD Battalion, 159th Combat Engineer Battalion and 509th Light Pontoon Company. The task force advanced rapidly up the peninsula to St Malo in mid-August, whence it proceeded to Brest, making

This photograph illustrates how the earth banks of the Normandy *bocage* inhibited the fire of tank destroyers. In such circumstances towed anti-tank guns were almost useless. (Imp. War Mus.)

One method of cutting through the banks was by attaching a 'rhino' device, here seen fitted to an M10. The 'rhino' was invented by Sgt. Curtis Culin, US Army, and prevented the vehicle's nose rising as it pushed its way through. Dozer blades were also attached to the M10 and M36. (US Army)

contact with 6th Armored Division, and later assisted in clearing the city itself.

The TD Group headquarters generally acted in an advisory capacity to their respective corps, although one Group HQ found itself running the Corps Rest Center! Occasionally Group HQs would command specific task forces, but these occasions were infrequent, and one example will suffice.

During the Roer River crossing on 23 February 1945 XIX Corps used the 2nd Tank Destroyer Group (702nd TD Bn. with M36s, and 801st TD Bn. with 3in towed guns) to provide neutralization and interdictory fire on targets up to 4,000 yards distant in supplement to the Corps' own artillery, with which the Group had established a fire control centre. The M36s fired at the rate of 100 rounds per hour per platoon, while the towed guns fired at 300 rounds per hour per company.

It might be expected that the Ardennes fighting provided numerous occasions involving the use of TD Groups, but the situation was so fluid that as TD units arrived they were pushed straight into the line, where they continued to write down the enemy's armour.

On 7 March 1945 the great railway bridge over the Rhine at Remagen was captured almost intact by a *coup de main*. Amongst the first troops rushed across to support the defenders of the shallow

bridgehead were the 899th Tank Destroyer Battalion; Company 'C' crossing on the 8th, and 'A' and 'B' two days later, all crossings being made under fire:

'The Germans fired direct at the bridge and the surrounding area on both sides of the river. It was a 'hot spot', and not a healthy one to be in for any length of time. As the TDs neared the river it was necessary to slow down, almost to a halt every few feet .... The bridge was hit often, but there was only a slight delay until it was cleared of wrecked vehicles and traffic continued once again. German planes came in at regular intervals, and all hell would break loose from the anti-aircraft units. If we weren't dodging Jerry's shells, bombs and strafings there was the falling ack-ack to put up with.'

For several days the Germans made fanatical attempts to throw the Americans back into the river. Then, as further bridgeheads were established elsewhere resistance collapsed, and the Allied armoured columns flowed across Germany. 1 May found the 899th on the Mulder River, waiting; in due course there appeared on the far bank hard-looking soldiers in worn, drab uniforms. They were Russians. For a day or two they were quite friendly...

The Pacific Theatre

In itself, Japanese armour posed no problem to American forces. On the other hand, 'The War Department felt growing concern over the large number of casualties experienced by units attacking Japanese fortifications. Leyte, Ie Shima and Okinawa were extremely costly in wounded and dead. Japanese field fortifications were mainly natural terrain barriers developed into intricate subterranean strongholds from which the Japanese would emerge and attack American units in the rear and on each flank. Cave openings were self-supporting and were so ably concealed that assault teams, after taking a frontal and/or reverse slope, would find that they had bypassed strongpoints from which a murderous fire all but wiped them out.'[1]

To combat this menace the Tank Destroyer Center set up a study unit known as the Sphinx Detachment, which had full-scale replicas of

[1] *Tank Destroyer History.*

An M10 crew at maintenance near Montcharivel, Normandy, subjected to banter from 6th Bn. Royal Scots Fusiliers, who seem to appreciate the skill with which the driver is using his 'tool, special adjusting'. (Imp. War Mus.)

Tank Destroyer success in combat

(1) Enemy losses incurred directly by action of TDF units, compiled from the after action reports of thirty-nine battalions serving in the European theatre. The figures are said to be incomplete, and are quoted from Study 60:

Tanks and SP guns: 1,344. Average battalion score, 34. Top score, 105
Armoured Cars and Heavy Vehicles: 251
Other Vehicles: 924
Anti-tank guns and other artillery pieces: 684
Pillboxes knocked out: 668
Machine Guns: 614
Aircraft shot down by organic AA weapons: 18. Top score, 5
Prisoners of War taken: 40,070. Top score, 5,421

(2) Analysis of kills scored by 899th Tank Destroyer Battalion in North Africa and Europe, from the unit history cited elsewhere:

Tanks:				
	PzKpfw III	8	*Anti-tank guns*	67
	PzKpfw IV	27	*Field Guns*	2
	Panther	32	*Aircraft*	4
	Tiger	1	*Pillboxes*	62
	Others	3	*Strongpoints*	15
Jagdpanther		7	*Machine gun nests*	93
Other SPs		15	*20mm AA guns*	20
Halftracks		10	*Observation posts*	7
Other vehicles		45	*Prisoners*	2,618

Other targets destroyed include a barracks, a factory and a flak tower.

Japanese positions built, and then established the best method of either demolishing them or at least sealing the cave entrances. Various types of projectile were used with fuses varying from instantaneous to .15 second delay, and it was found that the 90mm M36 produced the best results, with the 76mm M18 not far behind.

Since direct shooting was a TDF speciality, the majority of tank destroyer battalions in the Pacific theatre found themselves serving in an assault gun rôle, dealing with bunkers and cave entrances. This was not the rôle for which they had trained, but it saved their infantry comrades countless casualties.

British Service: Africa

When in 1940 the British Expeditionary Force was evacuated from France it left behind it no less than 509 2pdr. anti-tank guns which would have to be replaced immediately. The 2pdr. was also the principal British tank armament of the time; and although the more powerful 6pdr. design for both tank and anti-tank use was well advanced, the ordnance factories were forced to continue quantity production of the smaller gun for the immediate requirements of home defence. This decision, while inevitable in the circumstances, was to have disastrous effects for some years to come.

In the Western Desert the British forces in Egypt were faced with an invasion in strength from the Italian colonies in Libya. Anti-tank gunners, forced to tow the little 2pdrs. at speed over all sorts of going, found that the weapon's efficiency was becoming badly impaired by the constant battering, and urgently sought methods of reducing wear and tear whilst still maintaining mobility.

The answer appeared in the shape of the *portee*, said to be the invention of a Lieutenant Gillson, a Rhodesian officer.[1] The gun was mounted on the back of a cut-down lorry, usually a Chevrolet, and the idea was that it would be carried piggy-back fashion to the scene of action and there dismounted for use. In fact the gun was very rarely dismounted, first because time would not permit, and second because the mounting itself permitted a wide

[1]A variety of *portee* equipments were already in use in the United Kingdom, and had been produced to increase the mobility of response to the expected German landings.

An M36 involved in close quarter action in Brest, September 1944. The vehicle belongs to Company 'B', 705th Tank Destroyer Battalion, and carries a full set of unit markings. The 705th formed part of Third Army's Task Force 'A', which was commanded by HQ 1st Tank Destroyer Brigade. (US Army)

degree of traverse and the ammunition bins were located immediately behind the driver. The 2pdr. *portee* was the first British self-propelled anti-tank gun to see action, and was used extensively during the offensive which ejected the Italians first from Egypt and then from their own province of Cyrenaica.

The final action of this campaign, fought at Beda Fomm during the early days of February 1941, saw the *portees* being used in precisely the rôle which the United States Army intended for its own Tank Destroyer Force. The Italians, decisively beaten in the field at Sidi Barrani, had fallen back on their fortresses of Bardia and Tobruk, but each of these hollow refuges had been stormed, and what was left of their army was now retreating along the coast road through Benghazi towards Tripolitania.

Hoping to intercept them, Lt.-Gen. Richard O'Connor, commander of the British XIII Corps, despatched 7th Armoured Division through the difficult going of the Djebel Akhdar, so cutting across the base of the coastal bulge round which the Italians were moving. The division's advance guard, consisting of the armoured cars of the 11th Hussars, 2nd Battalion The Rifle Brigade, the 25pdrs. of 'C' Battery Royal Horse Artillery, and nine 37mm *portees* of 106th Royal Horse Artillery, emerged from the Djebel in the nick of time to establish a road block in the path of the retreating enemy.[1]

[1]A number of Bofors 37mm anti-tank *portees* were also in service at this period, but were withdrawn shortly afterwards. Both the 37mm and 2pdr. saw action at Beda Fomm.

The crews of 106th RHA, a Territorial regiment otherwise known as the Lancashire Yeomanry, snugged their *portees* down among the dunes on either side of the road, and were in action almost at once as the Italian advance guard drove up. Stalled, the column began launching a series of desperate attacks, accompanied by M13/40 tanks, hoping to smash its way through. By now, however, more and more Desert Rats were emerging from the Djebel, and although their petrol tanks were almost dry, they were fastening onto the flanks of the eleven-mile jam as well as reinforcing the block itself. For a day and a night the Italians struggled in the net, and made one last, brave attempt to break out on the morning of 7 February.

The weight of their attack fell mainly on 106th RHA, whose *portees* received the full benefit of the enemy's supporting artillery while the M13s surged forward. The attack was pressed home hard, and clearly the Italian tank men meant business as they began trading losses with the gun detachments. One gun commander calmly waited until the tanks had driven past his position and then shot six of them 'up the seat'; but one by one the little *portees* were wrecked until only one remained, manned by the battery commander, his batman and a cook. This drove out to a flank and destroyed the last Italian tanks as they drove onto the objective itself.

The Italians had played their last card. Everywhere men came forward to surrender, to the number of 25,000, leaving behind them over 200 guns and about 100 tanks, not all of which had been knocked out. The 106th RHA, which had done as much as any to '*Seek, Strike and Destroy*', claimed a total of twenty-seven tanks destroyed, and was awarded two Military Crosses, one Distinguished Conduct Medal and three Military Medals for its first action. Sad to relate, the unit was later all but destroyed fighting in Greece and Crete.

Without exception, British tank crews had the highest possible regard for the *portee* gunners, who fired steadily away from their exposed platforms with only the flimsy protection of the gun shield. Quite often 2pdr. *portees* would be found in action alongside the tanks; unlike their German opposite numbers manning the massive 88s, they could not lie back from the tank battle since they carried the same gun as the tanks themselves, and to get within killing range meant going forward into the very heart of the action.

Perhaps more than any other, the action fought by 'J' Battery 3rd Royal Horse Artillery at Sidi Rezegh epitomizes the spirit of the men who manned the *portees*. Operation 'Crusader', designed to effect the relief of beleaguered Tobruk, was in full swing, and the 7th Armoured Division's Support Group under Brigadier J. C. Campbell had taken possession of the escarpments around Sidi Rezegh. The Germans rightly regarded the area as a vital pivot of manoeuvre around which operations could be mounted to smash through their siege lines, and they were determined that the Support Group was going to be ejected from the position.

On the morning of 21 November 1941 the Support Group's artillery was deployed at the foot of the Upper Escarpment and completely dominated the Sidi Rezegh airfield. The 4th RHA were on the left, and in the centre was 60th Field Regiment RA, both equipped with 25pdrs., while on the right were the 2pdr. *portees* of 'J' Battery, 3rd RHA under the command of Major Bernard Pinney.

Pinney deployed his 'C' Troop, under Lieutenant Arthur Hardy, to cover the right flank of 60th Field, while 'A' Troop, commanded by Lieutenant Ward Gunn, was further still to the right. The Battery's third troop was retained as a mobile reserve.

At about 1130, after dive-bombing attacks and heavy shelling, the 21st Panzer Division began to advance against the Support Group, and the 25pdrs. went into action over open sights, using first High Explosive and then changing to Armour Piercing. This reaction was far more violent than anything the Germans had expected, and they were shaken to discover that a 25pdr. HE shell was quite capable of blowing the turret off a PzKpfw IV. Having already lost six tanks when still 2,000 yards from the objective, they halted and began to engage the distant gun lines with concentrated machine gun fire, while the PzKpfw IVs slammed over HE shells. The German artillery joined in and then their infantry mortar teams, until, as a Rifle Brigade officer put it, 'to look over the edge of a slit trench was suicidal'. The British artillery was dimly seen through a miasma of smoke, shell bursts and drifting dust, the red muzzle flashes showing that

Above: Crew of 75mm M3 halftrack of US Tank Destroyer Bn., Tunisia, winter 1942-43, in firing positions. Below: General arrangement of M3 halftrack hull with 75mm gun mounted.

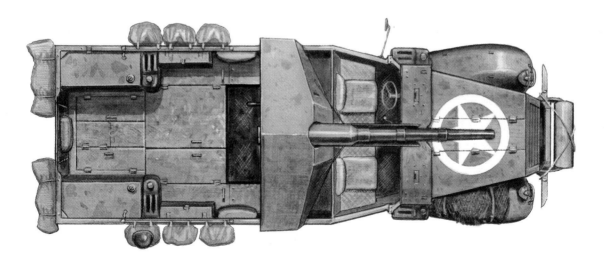

A

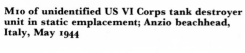

M10 of unidentified US VI Corps tank destroyer unit in static emplacement; Anzio beachhead, Italy, May 1944

M36 of US 705th Tank Destroyer Bn.; Brest, France, September 1944

B

M10 of Peloton de Commandement, 3e Escadron, Regt. Blindé de Fusiliers Marins, French 2e Division Blindé; Paris, France, summer 1944

M18 Hellcat of US 6th Tank Destroyer Group; Brest, France, August 1944

C

2pdr. portee of 3rd Royal Horse Artillery, British 7th Armoured Division; Western Desert, November 1941

D

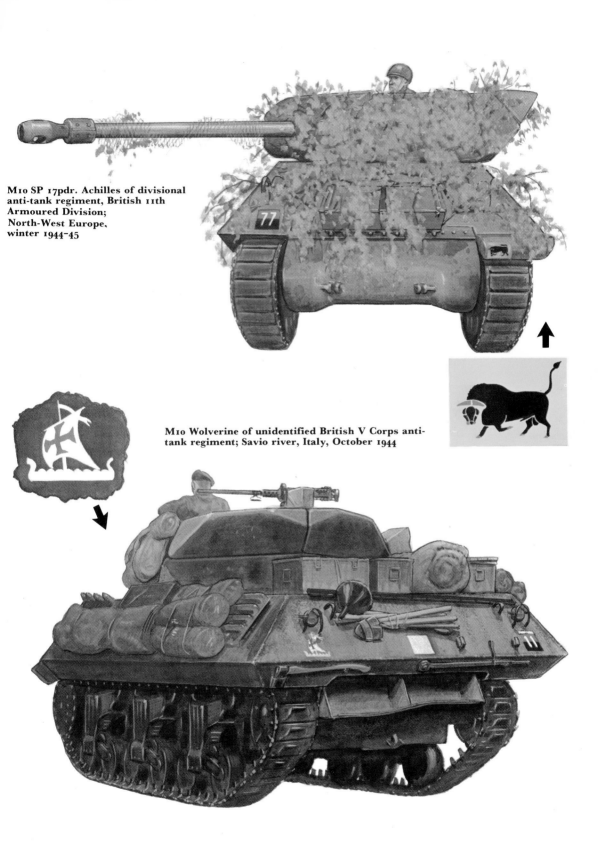

M10 SP 17pdr. Achilles of divisional anti-tank regiment, British 11th Armoured Division; North-West Europe, winter 1944–45

M10 Wolverine of unidentified British V Corps anti-tank regiment; Savio river, Italy, October 1944

E

a

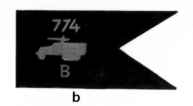

b

c

1   2   3

F

1 Bombardier, British Royal Horse Artillery; Western Desert, 1941
2 NCO Instructor, US Tank Destroyer Center; Camp Hood, 1942
3 Loader of M18 crew, 306th AT Co., US 77th Division; Okinawa, April 1945
4 Sergeant, Royal Artillery; North-West Europe, winter 1944-45
5 Quartier Maitre, Fusiliers Marins, 2e Division Blindé; France, 1944
6 Major, US 8th Tank Destroyer Group; Remagen bridgehead, Germany, March 1945
a Standard, US 644th TD Bn
b Guidon, Company 'B', US 774th TD Bn
c Pennant, US 8th TD Group
d Flag, US 6th TD Group

G

**SP 17pdr. Archer of 314 Battery, 105th AT Regt.
Royal Artillery, British V Corps; Italy, 1944**

**SP 17pdr. Archer of divisional AT regiment,
15th Scottish Division; North-West
Europe, winter 1944-45**

H

the gunners had not paused for an instant from the rhythm of their gun drill.

During all this Ward Gunn had been continually edging his four *portees* out towards the enemy, bringing them into killing range. They were spotted and the full fury of the Germans turned upon them. 'A' Troop began to fire back, the crews, according to a witness, completely composed, serving their guns, while their troop leader moved between them, directing and controlling. Watching Gunn through the all-enveloping smother, a Rifles' officer commented that 'never was there a clearer case of a man possessed with the joy of battle'.

Two of the *portees* were knocked out quickly by direct hits, but the two survivors continued to hit back with good results, to become the immediate focus of the Germans' attention. Spectators watched in fascinated horror as the detachments dropped one by one around the guns. A third *portee* was knocked out, but the last gun continued to fire until only one man was left, and he began to drive it out of action.

Some way behind, Gunn was talking to Pinney, who brusquely ordered him to stop the gun's withdrawal. The troop leader did so, and then manned the weapon himself after removing the dead crew. He was joined by Pinney, who almost at once was compelled to deal with a fire in an ammunition bin. While this raged Gunn kept on firing until struck in the head. He slumped dead, and Pinney, throwing away the fire extinguisher, dragged his body aside and continued to man the gun alone. It is not possible to estimate the enemy's loss, but when at last the Battery Commander drove the gun out, further hits having made it unusable, the two nearest tanks were certainly in flames.

Pinney drove straight to Hardy's 'C' Troop, now coming under intense pressure. Two of its *portees* had been knocked out, but the remaining two were pulling back slowly onto the flank of 60th Field, concentrating their fire on some German tanks which were trying to work round the position. After the two leading Panzers had been knocked out the remainder withdrew, and the crisis of the battle had passed.

Both Gunn and Pinney were recommended for the award of the Victoria Cross; it was given only to Gunn, posthumously. The morning after the action Pinney was killed by a stray shell. In recognition of its heroic service his Battery was awarded that rarest of artillery distinctions, an Honour Title, and is now known as 'J' (Sidi Rezegh) Battery, Royal Horse Artillery.[1]

The Middle Years: Italy

During the immediate post-Dunkirk period, analysis of the events in France had led to recommendations that each corps should have an anti-tank regiment at the direct disposal of the corps commander, and that one battery of the Divisional anti-tank regiments should be self-propelled.

By September 1941 the General Staff was warming very slowly to the concept of the self-propelled anti-tank gun, but in spite of the benefits which had arisen from the aggressive use of *portees* in the Western Desert, it still envisaged a largely defensive rôle for such weapons, in direct contrast to the United States Army's policy. However, it was conceded that self-propelled anti-tank guns permitted longer marches than could be achieved with towed guns; that they had a better cross-country performance; that they were valuable hit and run weapons; and that such equipment enabled reserve guns to be deployed rapidly. It went on to suggest the fitting of a 2pdr. to a Loyd carrier in such a manner as to permit 225 degrees of traverse, the idea being that these vehicles would equip one quarter of the divisional anti-tank regiment's strength as well as the anti-tank platoons of the divisional reconnaissance regiments. Only a very few were ever built, although the Australian Army produced its own variation on the same theme.[2]

By mid-1942 the long-awaited 6pdr. was beginning to arrive on the battlefield. A number of batteries carried this *en portee*, but as it was a much larger gun than the 2pdr., it was not as convenient, and tended to be dismounted more often before going into action. These were later supplemented, or replaced, by an armoured version known as the Deacon, in which the gun was housed inside a

[1]Only five such titles were awarded for service during World War II. 106th RHA's action at Beda Fomm did not contain all the circumstances required by the very strict rules governing such awards.
[2]*Development of Artillery Tactics and Equipment 1939–45*. Interestingly, the Germans mounted a 37mm anti-tank gun on captured Loyd carriers.

A British M10 Wolverine supports infantry consolidating newly-won ground during the Gothic Line fighting in Italy, 1944. (Imp. War Mus.)

turret mounted on an AEC Matador lorry. This arrangement permitted very little traverse, but as the gun engaged 'over the tail' further traverse was quickly obtainable by getting the driver to swing the vehicle in the required direction. The Deacons were usually issued on the scale of one battery per anti-tank regiment, and their official rôle was that of mobile anti-tank reserve. By June 1943 they were becoming obsolete and were beginning to be replaced by American M10s, for which an initial order of 1,500 had been placed.

Meanwhile work was proceeding on the production of the first British tracked tank destroyer to enter service, the Archer. This consisted of the excellent 17pdr. anti-tank gun mounted on the chassis of the now-obsolete Valentine Infantry Tank. While the fighting compartment was housed at the front of the vehicle, the long gun pointed over the tail, and consequently the equipment had to be reversed into its firing position. In position, the driver became an ammunition number of necessity, as the breech recoiled directly over his seat. Traverse was limited to 11 degrees either side of the centre line, but could be supplemented by moving the vehicle.

Archers began reaching the line in October 1944, and as their numbers began to increase many

M10s were withdrawn so that their 3in guns could be replaced with the more powerful 17pdrs. In this composite version of the M10, known in British service as the Achilles, the breech-heavy piece was balanced by a counter-weight mounted immediately behind the muzzle brake.

British thinking on tank destroyers was now firmly set. 'In contrast to the American policy, the idea of seeking out and destroying enemy armour was discouraged. A suitable rôle for the SP anti-tank gun, it was thought, was the engagement of tanks that stood off and neutralized our forward localities; or when employed with armoured formations, to help in the defence of pivots or localities held by the infantry.'[1]

This bald statement perhaps sounds a trifle stuffy but it must be remembered that the days of the massed tank attack were over in the Mediterranean. In Tunisia, Sicily and Italy the Germans fought defensive actions in mountainous country, and in Italy in particular the self-propelled gun played a dominant rôle in defence. An SP surrounded by half a dozen machine gun posts, would often wait in concealment and not open fire until the Allied tanks were within a point-blank 100 yards; then, having destroyed two or three, it would make its escape.

'What was needed was a weapon that could move across country by a covered route to a position from which enemy tanks could be engaged by surprise. For lack of it, anti-tank protection had become perhaps the most important rôle for tanks in support of infantry.[2]

In fact the M10s and Archers provided such a weapon, and the result was an extremely tight battlefield interlock of all arms involved in an attack. The tanks dealt with the enemy's infantry and machine gun posts; the infantry dealt with fixed anti-tank guns and *panzerfaust* teams; the field artillery, through its Forward Observation Officers, would lay on immediate concentrations as required; and the tank destroyers, lying back in good overshoot positions, would deal with any enemy armour which tried to intervene. In the consolidation phase the tank destroyers might also dig in on the captured ground until the infantry's own guns could be brought up.

[1]*Development of Artillery Tactics and Equipment 1939–45.*
[2]*Ibid.*

There is the wary tension of men still under fire about these infantrymen moving slowly into Fontainebleau on 23 August 1944. The rapid advance had stretched even radio communications to the limit, as the amount of aerial being carried by the M10 shows. (US Army)

A good example of these highly developed minor tactics is an incident which occurred on the afternoon of 4 September 1944 during the Gothic Line fighting. The infantry battalion, the Canadian 48th Highlanders, had been stalled by enfiladed machine gun fire; their supporting armour, Churchills of 'B' Squadron 48th Royal Tank Regiment, was unable to deal with the problem since the tanks were themselves stalled by what were believed to be German SPs. In support was a nine-gun battery of M10s (not identified) and a field battery of 105mm guns. It was decided that while the M10s engaged the SPs, the tanks would take out the machine gun positions, following which the infantry would continue their advance.

'The M10s were manoeuvred carefully into fire positions to take on the SP guns. The SP on the right was observed to be a Panther and the range 2,000 yards. It was engaged and moved off at once,

first behind a house and later into some trees. The M10s fired about a dozen rounds and the 105s fired to encourage him to move into view again. What success was achieved is hard to say, but later two brewed-up Panthers were examined in the area. The gun or tank on the left could not be observed so we put down a concentration of 105s on the suspected area.'[1]

The Italian campaign had become a killing match between skilled teams of professionals, but now that they had been properly equipped, batteries like 314th Anti-Tank, which had grimly reversed their little *portees* into the heart of numerous tank battles without much hope of

[1]General Account of Operations from August 28th to September 23rd, 48 RTR.

27

In addition to cratering roads in the path of the advancing Allied armies, the Germans mined the verges, so that once a by-pass had been cleared it had to be stuck to. (Imp. War Mus.)

survival, now looked forward to the prospect of action. During this same period an engagement took place when sharp eyes in one of 314th Battery's Archers detected a Tiger, and the 17pdr. lashed back on recoil. The round missed narrowly, but the crack of heavy, high-velocity shot is instantly recognizable, and the German tank commander at once swung his huge vehicle out of sight behind a building. Unfortunately for him the Tiger was spotted by a Lysander Air OP, which signalled its whereabouts. The Archer fired again and the 17pdr. shot slammed straight through the building and the tank's thin side armour as well. It was with considerable pleasure that the gunners inspected the wreck some days later.

Firing High Explosive, the tank destroyers also acted as reinforcing artillery, a rôle in which they served in all theatres of war, but which was initially developed on a large scale during the first year of the Italian campaign. Sometimes the firing was

Direct, that is with the target in sight, but by clamping a Gunner's Quadrant onto the breech and using the traverse indicator it was also possible to undertake Indirect fire, in which the fall of shot was corrected by a distant observer until the target was struck. Once targets had been acquired and the relevant elevation and traverse angles registered on a range card, they could be engaged by night as well as by day.

Normandy and North-West Europe

Back in the United Kingdom, as training proceeded for the invasion of Europe, it was becoming quite apparent that in certain circumstances the tank destroyer held the key to success. Everyone agreed that the German reaction to the landings would probably take the form of a series of massive armoured counter-attacks. There was also general agreement that as the towed 17pdr. anti-tank gun was awkward to handle, difficulties could be

An M36 of 607th Tank Destroyer Battalion in Metz, 20 November 1944. (US Army)

Equipment history of 105th Anti-Tank Regiment, Royal Artillery—a Corps anti-tank regiment:

1941–42   Western Desert   2pdr. *portee*
314 Battery of this regiment accompanied 7th Armoured Brigade to Burma, and was forced to destroy its *portees* during the retreat to India. It subsequently returned to the Middle East via India and Iraq.

1942–43	Western Desert, Tunisia	2 batteries 6pdr. *portee*
		2 batteries Deacon
1943	Sicily	2 batteries 17pdr. towed
		2 batteries 6pdr. towed
Early 1944	Italy	2 batteries M10
		1 battery 17pdr. towed
		1 battery 6 pdr. towed
Late 1944–45	Italy	2 batteries Archer
		1 battery M10
		1 battery 17pdr. towed

Battery establishment in the period 1944–45 was twelve guns.

anticipated in getting it across the beaches and emplaced in the line in adequate time. It was decided that the anti-tank regiments of those divisions which carried out the assault landings would be equipped with a proportion of M10s, which could simply motor out of their LCTs and form an immediate anti-tank gun screen where required. That armoured counter-attacks did not immediately develop on the scale expected was largely the fault of Adolf Hitler.

The nature of the Normandy *bocage* imposed much the same sort of fighting that was taking place in Italy, with the M10s providing direct fire support for infantry/tank operations. 'It was as important as ever to get anti-tank guns forward quickly to a captured objective; all the more so because of the inadequate killing power of the Churchill tank. The towed 17pdr. was not easy to manoeuvre and it was often twelve to fifteen hours before it could be dug in ready for action in the new position. Hence it was decided to perpetuate the SP

In response the Germans, already well aware of the M10's primary weakness, began subjecting tank destroyer crews to air-burst shelling against which even well emplaced vehicles could offer little defence. Not surprisingly, demands were made for splinter-proof overhead cover, but beyond the production of a few mock-ups, nothing was done.

On 8 July 1944 a battery of 62nd Anti-Tank Regiment RA fought a spectacular action in the manner for which their vehicles had originally been designed. The battery concerned had supported an infantry/tank attack on the village of Buron, and by 0900 all seemed to be over; however, as the War Diary recounts, it was not.

'At about 0900 the infantry (the Highland Light Infantry of Canada) had taken Buron though there were several Germans still holding out at the far end of the village. The battery moved up, and 'B' Troop were deployed on the south-east side of the village and 'A' Troop at the south and west of the village. Shortly afterwards the Germans put down a very heavy shelling and mortar barrage and quickly followed this up by a counter-attack of some twenty or thirty tanks. Two guns of 'B' Troop were able to engage, and between them accounted for some twelve to thirteen Panthers and Mark IVs. The remaining tanks then withdrew to the south-east. The guns which accounted for the tanks were

element introduced into anti-tank units for the initial landings. In future, infantry divisional anti-tank batteries were to consist of one troop 17pdr. towed, one troop 17pdr. Wolverine (sic) or M10, and one troop 6pdr. towed. The idea was that the 6pdr. or SP 17pdr. should be used as the FDL (Forward Defended Locality) gun, with the towed 17pdr. acting as a 'long stop'.'[1]

A 17pdr. Achilles of 11th Armoured Division's anti-tank regiment in action against a pillbox on the German frontier, 11 October 1944. (Imp. War Mus.)

[1]*Development of Artillery Tactics and Equipment 1939–45.*

(commanded by) Sgt. H. W. Bowden and Sgt. G. P. J. Donovan.'

The battery had not got off lightly, and after the action only three of its Achilles were in a fit state to continue. There was also an interesting sequel. 'On a subsequent visit by the Prime Minister, the victims were shown to him as the bag of our Shermans and it took some effort on the part of Second Army to adjust our claim.'[1]

During subsequent operations in Belgium, Holland and Germany the British tank destroyers, in addition to their other duties, often acted as heavyweight snipers, moving into position before the start of an attack to take out potential enemy observation posts in the church steeples and windmills that dominated the flat landscape.[2]

[1] *Royal Artillery Commemoration Book.*
[2] A case of history repeating itself. In 1917 Cdr. Oliver Locker-Lampson's No. 1 Squadron RNACD, struggling to hold a 25-mile gap in the line abandoned by the disintegrating Russian Army, had used their 3pdr. Seabrook Heavies in just this rôle.

Another Achilles of the same unit. Gun barrels of this length stick out like very sore thumbs, and their outline must be broken up if the vehicle is sited in a concealed firing position; hence the chicken wire sleeve behind the counter-weight. (Imp. War Mus.)

The period June 1944 to May 1945 saw the high-water mark of British tank destroyer usage. Although a fully turreted version, the Charioteer, mounting a 20pdr. gun on a Cromwell tank chassis, entered service during the early 1950s, by then tanks were themselves mounting such heavy armament that the need for tank destroyers as a separate family had ceased to exist. Thus the fundamental question was resolved; in future it would be the tank that would concentrate on the destruction of its own kind.

Perhaps it would be as well to leave the story at a high point in Royal Artillery history—its greatest bombardment of World War II, fired in support of Operation 'Veritable', better known as the Battle of the Reichswald. Participating in an HE Indirect fire 'Pepperpot' group were the Archers of 20th Anti-Tank Regiment RA, whose commanding officer has left a vivid word picture of the occasion:

'Fifteen seconds to go . . . ten . . . five. There goes one of my SP troops; they're a few seconds early—not that you'd notice it, because almost immediately the sky seems crammed with tracer. Bofors pumping away from in front, from the sides and over our heads from behind. With their flat trajectory they seem to be skimming the housetops. The 17pdrs. have a more sober air as, with reduced charge and comparatively high trajectory they sail gracefully away into the night sky, the tracer burning out long before the round falls. I am quite certain of one thing; our war correspondents will run out of adjectives long before we run out of ammunition. It is terrific; by far the best thing I've ever seen. More impressive than D-Day—and makes Crystal Palace seem like table fireworks.' (Lt.-Col. G. B. Thatcher, DSO, in *The Royal Artillery Commemoration Book*.)

M10s at speed in the Huertgen Forest, 18 November 1944. (US Army)

Basic ballistic data of anti-tank guns mentioned in text:

British	*Weight of shot*	*Muzzle Velocity*
2pdr.	2.5lb	2800ft/sec
6pdr.	6.0lb	2700ft/sec
17pdr.	17.0lb	2900ft/sec
American		
37mm M3	1.61lb	2600ft/sec
75mm M1897A	14.6lb	1950ft/sec
3in M7	12.65lb	2800ft/sec
76mm M1 series	15.5lb	2600ft/sec
90mm M3	23.4lb	2800ft/sec

It is interesting to note that during the relevant period increase in weight of shot was preferred to increased muzzle velocity as a means of better tank killing. Effective range varied from 600 yards (2pdr. and 37mm) to 2,000 yards (17pdr. and 90mm), but kills were regularly recorded above these figures, particularly in cases where the enemy's thinner side or rear armour had been penetrated. There are many imponderables in anti-tank gunnery, not least of which are the angle and point of impact.

British and American Tank Destroyers

BRIEF TECHNICAL DETAILS

Archer
Length: 21′ 11″
Height: 7′ 4½″
Width: 8′ 7½″
Weight: 16 tons
Armour: 60mm max.
Armament: 1 × 17pdr.
Speed: 15mph max.
Ammunition stowage: 39 rounds
Crew: 4

Achilles
Armament: 1 × 17pdr. otherwise as M10

Gun Motor Carriage M10
Length: 19′ 7″
Height: 8′ 1½″
Width: 10′ 0″
Weight: 29.4 tons
Armour: 37mm max.
Armament: 1 × 3in M7
Speed: 30mph max.
Ammunition stowage: 54 rounds
Crew: 5

Gun Motor Carriage M36
Length: 20′ 2″
Height: 8′ 11″
Width: 10′ 0″
Weight: 28.1 tons
Armour: 50mm max.
Armament: 1 × 90mm M3
Speed: 30mph max.
Ammunition stowage: 47 rounds
Crew: 5

Gun Motor Carriage M18
Length: 17′ 4″
Height: 7′ 9″
Width: 9′ 9″
Weight: 18.25 tons
Armour: 12mm max.
Armament: 1 × 76mm M1
Speed: 50mph max.
Ammunition stowage: 45 rounds
Crew: 5

The Plates

A: Crew positions and general interior arrangement, 75mm M3 halftrack

The crew are depicted at the moment of opening fire, and we take their positions from photographs in a US Army manual. The gunner crouches on the left of the breech at the sights, and is about to give the command to fire. The assistant gunner stands, cramped under the cover of the gunshield, on the right; he has pulled the lanyard, and awaits the gunner's command before releasing it to fire the gun. The loader is forced to grovel on the deck to keep clear of the recoil of the weapon, which frequently caught unwary loaders, with painful results. The ammunition stowage was beneath the breech, with three rows of stowage 'pipes' for rounds; these were staggered, six above seven above six. The top row can be seen; the other two rows were below the main deck level, accessible only because a well in the deck gave access. The tip-up seats can be seen on the hull interior walls on each side; crew accommodation was extremely basic. The lower painting shows from above the general interior arrangement, with the tip-up seats on the side walls and rear hull door and the access well for the ammunition stowage.

B (top) M10 of unidentified US VI Corps tank destroyer unit; Anzio beachhead, Italy, May 1944

A photograph of this vehicle appears in the accompanying pages. The markings are interesting, as is the use of Olive Drab in conjunction with Earth Yellow in a faded and indistinct camouflage scheme. Such paint jobs were sometimes seen in Sicily and Italy, although not often as late as this. The plethora of white stars indicates a certain anxiety as to Allied troops' standards of vehicle recognition, and the large white area on the rear of the turret probably had the same purpose. Such

M36s of 703rd Tank Destroyer Battalion moving into position in support of 82nd Airborne Division during the Ardennes fighting. Note absence of unit markings and visible stars. (US Army)

precautions obviously negate the usefulness of the camouflage painting, and give excellent aiming marks for German gunners. Note the fairly uncommon application of an individual tactical number—'8'; and the mounting of two .50 cal. machine guns, one at the front and one at the rear of the turret.

B (bottom) M36 of 705th TD Bn. US 3rd Army; Brest, France, September 1944

Again, this painting is an interpretation of one of the accompanying photos. The plain overall Olive Drab paint job is entirely typical of armoured vehicles in the European theatre, as is the relative obscurity of the white Allied recognition star. Note typically heavy stowage of crew packs and bedrolls, jerrycans, cable reels, etc. around the outside of the turret. The application and retention of full unit codes in the front line is not so typical. They follow the regulation sequence: '3A' for US 3rd Army, '705 TD' identifying the battalion, and 'B-14' identifying company and vehicle. In units under Corps or Army command the first code (e.g. '3A', or 'II' for II Corps) replaced the usual divisional code (e.g. '2 triangle' for 2nd Armored Division).

M10s firing in the indirect rôle at night. The occasion is an operational test of high/low flash propellants. The vehicle on the left is using standard ammunition, which produced a brilliant white muzzle flash, while that on the right is using a specially prepared charge which gave only a dull, red glow. (US Army)

M36 in snow camouflage shortly after the 'Battle of the Bulge'. (US Army)

C (top) M10, Peloton de Commandement. 3ᵉ Escadron, Regt. Blindé de Fusiliers Marins, French 2ᵉ Division Blindé; Paris, summer 1944

The famous 'Division Leclerc' included representatives of many Free French units, and the self-propelled tank destroyers were crewed by sailors of the Fusiliers Marins. After escaping from occupied France at various times from June 1940 onwards, these seamen led a checkered career. At one point they provided the anti-aircraft crews for the garrison of Bir Hakeim in the Libyan desert; incorporated into the premier Free French formation for the liberation of their homeland, they commemorated their origins by painting the names of their former vessels on their armoured vehicles, e.g. 'Flibustier'. The divisional insignia was the cross of Lorraine on a map of France, in white and blue as illustrated, on both forward hull sides. The French tricolour was painted on the hull sides of most Free French AFVs, usually to the rear, and sometimes with a yellow outer rim. The tactical sign ahead of it is typical of French practice at this time. Each major unit of the division was identified

by a letter—here, 'Y'. The company was identified by the number of uprights on the bar, whose position above, below, or vertically at either side of the regimental letter indicated the platoon. A French serial number has replaced the US number, painted in white 'Cyrillic' numerals on the front glacis and always preceded by a small, narrow tricolour. Allied recognition stars are retained. The crew wear US uniforms with French headgear and insignia. Seamen retained their bonnets, petty officers and officers their peaked caps; officers seem often to have worn the French armoured troops helmet of pre-war vintage, in khaki with brown leather furniture (see Plate F/G fig. 5).

C (bottom) M18 Hellcat of US 6th Tank Destroyer Group; Brest, France, August 1944

Photographed during the winkling-out of the German garrison of Brest in the summer of 1944, this example of the fast and deadly Hellcat bears rather more in the way of individual crew insignia than one normally sees in front-line photos. The name DON'T WANT'A is painted in small white capitals low on the hull side centrally, and further forward is a swim-suited pin-up. We have made an educated guess at the colours and design of this pin-up, judging from the tones and outline of the necessarily small and blurred monochrome photo-

The wrecked jeep, casualties, and infantrymen sprinting for the cover of the tank destroyer emphasize the fanatical quality of German resistance in some areas: Schillingen, 15 March 1945. (US Army)

graph from which we worked. Crossed legs would seem to be logical, given the name. . . . There are two staggered lines of white lettering to the left of the girl's head; these may be a repetition of the vehicle name, but cannot be made out clearly in the photo. The vehicle serial number is clearly marked—often it was painted over or allowed to wear off in the front line. The bridge classification code is presented on a yellow disc on the hull front cheek plate, probably on one side only.

D: 2 pdr. portee of 3rd Royal Horse Artillery, British 7th Armoured Division; Western Desert, November 1941

Two views of the equipment made famous by 'A' Troop, 'J' Battery, 3rd RHA on 21 November 1941 at Sidi Rezegh, where Lt. Ward Gunn won a posthumous Victoria Cross in the action described in the body of the text. The typical stowage would be heavier and more varied, as the vehicles of old desert hands were liberally stacked with bedrolls, jerrycans, oil and water cans, small arms ammunition boxes used for crew kit, packs, greatcoats, camouflage netting, ration boxes, tarpaulins, and personal weapons. We have limited the stowage the better to show details of the rather complex 2pdr. gun and its Chevrolet-built Canadian Military Pattern 3-tonner. Markings are limited to the divisional sign, presented on a single plate (typically of 7th Armoured Division) with the tactical sign—the Royal Artillery's red-over-blue, with the white '55' carried at that period by vehicles of the

divisional anti-tank regiment. Some, but not all *portees* had a white serial number marked high and centrally on the cab doors, apparently 'L' followed by seven digits. The lieutenant sighting the gun in the lower view wears a typical (but purely speculative) combination of regimental No. 1 Dress cap—a frequent affectation by officers of 'mounted' regiments at that time—with battledress blouse and KD slacks. The crewman in the upper view wears standard KD shirt and shorts with the khaki Field Service cap.

E (top) M10 SP 17pdr. Achilles of divisional anti-tank regiment RA, British 11th Armoured Division; North-West Europe, winter 1944–45

The photo of this vehicle which accompanies the body of the text shows typical stowage when unobscured by foliage. It was highly characteristic of Allied armoured vehicles in the often close country of France and Germany to concentrate attached foliage, scrim-net and chicken wire camouflage on the turret and upper part of the hull—the areas most frequently exposed to the enemy's view above hedges and banks. The long 17pdr. gun of the Achilles, with its prominent counterweight and muzzle brake, was a prime identification feature, and was often swathed in chicken wire or hessian. The markings are absolutely regulation—the divisional sign of 11th Armoured, a black bull on yellow, on the near side front and off side rear; and the tactical sign of the armoured division's integral anti-tank regiment, by now a white '77' on the red-over-blue RA flash, in the opposite positions. Loss of a track guard has apparently led to repainting of the latter on this vehicle. The accompanying photo confirms that no other markings were carried on the turret or hull sides, not even the Allied star. The crewman wears the rimless Royal Armoured Corps steel helmet.

E (bottom) M10 Wolverine of unidentified British V Corps anti-tank regiment RA; Savio River, Italy, October 1944

Again, from one of the accompanying photographs, this painting shows the heavy stowage typical of front-line vehicles. Apart from bedrolls, tarpaulins, ammunition boxes, spare track links, buckets and fuel funnel, this vehicle carries a

The last lap. Airborne Engineers repair a blown bridge for the passage of an Achilles tank destroyer: Coesfeld, 30 March 1945. (Imp. War Mus.)

M18s of Company 'B', 637th Tank Destroyer Battalion, engaging Japanese positions dug into the hills of Luzon, Philippine Islands. (US Army)

bundle of stakes and several picks and shovels at the rear, for the use of accompanying infantry when consolidating captured positions—a rôle in which SP anti-tank guns and infantry often co-operated in this theatre. Another photo of the same vehicle from the front shows the full markings, which were repeated exactly on the rear: the V Corps sign on the left as viewed; a white square—probably a convoy station-keeping device—centrally; and the regimental flash on the right. This latter is the red-

blue RA flash with the number '11', and the white top bar of Corps troops. An additional marking sometimes carried on the solid top decking at the front of the turret was a British air recognition sign, in the form of the RAF roundel—red centre, white ring, blue ring, and thin yellow outer rim.

F/G: Crew uniforms and unit flags:

1 Bombardier, Royal Horse Artillery; Western Desert, 1941

This 'desert scruff' wears a typical combination of garments. The khaki greatcoat has been cut down into a 'shortie'; on the shoulder-straps are the black-on-khaki regimental tabs which officially replaced metal or coloured cloth shoulder titles at the beginning of the war—here, 'RHA'. The Field Service cap, with the RA's bomb and scroll badge, is carried under the shoulder-strap; and the bombardier's chevrons appear on both upper arms. KD shirt and slacks and khaki wool sweater are set off by a touch of 'swank' in the form of the

The M18 commander provides covering fire with his machine gun as infantry run for cover. It was common practice for the Japanese to allow troops to pass their position before opening fire from the rear. Baguio, Luzon, 24 April 1945. (US Army)

regimentally coloured 'stable belt'. He carries his basic web equipment, which, typically for the type of unit and the period, includes the old '08 clip pouches.

2 Technical Sergeant, Instruction Staff, US Tank Destroyer Center; Camp Hood, 1942

The ubiquitous overall of light Olive Drab twill in a herringbone pattern was the basis of the US vehicle crewman's working kit. It is worn here with the summer 'chino' version of the 'overseas cap', piped around the turn-up with branch-colour cord. At this date Tank Destroyer enlisted men wore an unofficial piping reflecting their all-arms origins, in a 'twist' pattern of repeated yellow-red-blue, for the cavalry, artillery, and infantry. In March 1943 the branch was officially authorized a piping of black and golden orange in alternating twist. Rank chevrons in light Olive Drab on midnight blue appear on both upper sleeves.

3 Loader, M18 crew, 306th AT Co., US 77th Division: Okinawa, April 1945

From a photograph of a crew re-ammunitioning with 76mm AP rounds, this painting shows the two-piece faded Olive Drab fatigues which formed the basis of most combat uniforms in the Pacific theatre, worn in combination with the US leather tank crew helmet. The rather archaic-looking goggles are interesting—the big rubber-rimmed single-lens type worn by the preceding figure are much more common in photos. The trouser legs are rolled high over standard russet leather double-buckle combat boots. The gunnery gloves are worn

to prevent handling accidents caused by sweating palms, and were indispensable when clearing hot expended cases from the turret floor. In action many loaders preferred to work without gloves, but they were not such an encumbrance as the painting might suggest, as American loaders used their balled fist for ramming, this being knocked clear by the closing breech-block. British loaders preferred to use a hard back-hand sweep, which was faster and which kept fingers out of the danger area; use of the fingers of the forehand (i.e. that nearest the rear of the gun) was likely to result in their neat and rapid severance between the breech-block and chamber.

4 Sergeant, Royal Artillery SP AT regiment, XXX Corps; North-West Europe, winter 1944–45

This Achilles commander is returning from a foraging or barter expedition among the friendly Dutch with his Royal Armoured Corps helmet full of spuds, and a stone bottle of 'Geneva' to wash them down. His 'beret'—actually, the General Service cap which replaced the Field Service cap in 1943—bears the RA bomb and scroll badge. Over his battledress he wears the popular leather jerkin worn by most British soldiers in both World Wars, and the absolute minimum of webbing in the form of his belt alone. Vehicle crews shunned webbing for fear of catching it on protrusions if forced to bail out of a burning vehicle in a hurry. At the top of the blouse sleeve is the XXX Corps sign—a black boar on a white disc on a black square—and below it the RA arm of service flash. Sergeants of Royal Artillery wore the regiment's cannon badge above their rank chevrons on both sleeves. A slung Sten gun is a typical vehicle commander's weapon when wandering about in the open.

5 Quartier Maitre 1e Classe, Regt. Blindé de Fusiliers Marins, French 2e Division Blindé; France, summer 1944

This junior petty officer, lugging a box of belted .50 cal. ammunition back to his M10, wears almost entirely US issue clothing; the American Army took over the outfitting and arming of the Free French forces in 1943, while the British Army provided the same services for the Belgians and Dutch. The M1941 field jacket is worn over the one-piece herringbone twill vehicle overall and an

Olive Drab wool shirt. The headgear and insignia are French; the sailor's bonnet, doubtless treasured during the regiment's long wanderings since 1940, bears the cap tally 'FUSILIERS MARINS'. The three red chevrons of this rank are worn on a midnight-blue slip-on on both shoulder-straps; and the crossed foul anchors in red on a blue square were the insignia of all active naval units in 'the fleet'. US boots and webbing complete the uniform.

6 Major, US 8th Tank Destroyer Group; Remagen bridgehead, Germany, March 1945
Taken from published reminiscences of a Group veteran, this figure wears the tan windcheater 'tanker's jacket' with knit waist, collar and cuffs; US crews of SP guns in Europe seem to have worn combinations of infantry and tank clothing indiscriminately, but the popular tank jacket was much in demand. Since it has no shoulder-straps, the major's leaf insignia is sewn to the shoulder on a leather patch. The Tank Destroyer Force shoulder patch is worn high on the left sleeve only: it is repeated in detail on the back cover of this book. The cavalry yellow scarf betrays this officer's previous branch. The proofed M1943 combat trousers are tucked into strapped leather boots with composition soles—probably cut-down modifications of pre-war field boots. Full basic combat webbing is worn, and an M1 carbine is carried as well as a holstered .45 pistol. The helmet markings are most interesting: on the front, a decal of the TD Force insignia, above a brazed-on major's rank leaf; on each side, a decal of the Group's pennant, point upwards, in orange and black; on the back centrally, the white vertical bar indicating an Officer.

a Battalion standard, US 644th TD Bn. The battalion badge, a spiked gauntlet, is just visible on the central panel on the eagle's chest.
b Guidon of Co. 'B', US 774th TD Bn. In the branch's colours of orange and black, with a stylized 75mm M3 halftrack device, this guidon measured 2ft 3¾in long by 1ft 8in deep overall.
c Pennant of US 8th TD Group, March 1945. The 1944 version was in black and orange only, the shape being a stylized representation of the cross-section of an AP shell with a false ogive. The red section

was added over half of the black as a compliment to the attachment of the 281st Field Artillery Bn. to the Group in the Remagen bridgehead in March 1945. Other Group units were the 629th, 656th, 814th, 817th, 893rd and 899th TD Bns; two troops of 14th Cavalry; and 16th Belgian Fusilier Bn.
d Flag of US 6th TD Group, 1944. Overall dimension, 4ft long and 3ft deep.

H (top) SP 17pdr. Archer of 314 Battery, 105th AT Regt. RA, British V Corps; Italy, 1944

Front—travelling—view of the Archer. In contrast to the overall dark olive green of the other British vehicles depicted, this gun sports the alternative colour for the Italian front, officially described as 'light mud'. Markings are limited to the serial and the vehicle name, 'DEFIANT'.

H (bottom) SP 17pdr. Archer of divisional AT regiment RA, 15th Scottish Division; North-West Europe, winter 1944–45

Rear—business end!—view of the Archer; note extra rail welded across rear deck to hold jerrycans, etc. The RA flash bears the '46' of an infantry division's integral AT regiment. The central marking, a blue square with a red corner, is the battery/troop identification, the red corner moving around the square according to the troop. The divisional sign is on the right.

The last of the big-gun tank destroyers, the Charioteer, could offer no improvement upon the fire-power available to contemporary battle tanks. (RAC Tank Museum)

Notes sur les planches en couleur

A Le canonnier (à gauche) donne l'ordre de tirer; son second (à droite) se prépare à actionner le mécanisme de tir, tandis que le chargeur (premier plan) s'aplatit pour être hors de portée du mouvement de recul de la culasse. On distingue les trois rangées de 'tubes' d'entrepôt des munitions, dont deux sont enfouis dans un 'puits' situé sous le pont du véhicule. La seconde illustration nous montre la disposition intérieure générale du véhicule, avec le 'puits' dans la partie sombre.

B (en haut) La couleur des véhicules blindés US n'était pas toujours *Olive Drab* unie—en Sicile ou en Italie, comme ici, le revêtement de camouflage des véhicules comportait d'ordinaire une teinte plus pâle. Le nombre des étoiles blanches qui figurent sur ce M10 indique la nervosité de l'équipage redoutant quelque erreur d'identification de la part de canonniers amis! **(en bas)** Revêtement uni typique *Olive Drab*, dans une certaine mesure peu courant, parce que les véhicules des lignes de front ne portaient pas souvent l'ensemble des inscriptions d'identification règlementaires de l'unité. Ces inscriptions désignent: '3A' = US 3rd Army; '705TD' = le bataillon; 'B-14' = la compagnie, ainsi que le véhicule individuel.

C (en haut) Les célèbres Fusiliers Marins peignaient le nom de leurs anciens bateaux sur leurs M10s. Le 'Y' désigne le régiment de la division; les trois barres verticales, l'escadre; la position des barres d'escadre, le peloton; et la carte de France avec, par-dessus, la croix de Lorraine, est l'insigne de la division. **(en bas)** L'inscription: 'Don't Want 'A' (On n'en veut pas), ainsi que la pin-up en maillot, sont l'œuvre de l'équipage. Le '16' correspond à une classification de poids permettant le passage des ponts.

D Véhicule du régiment qui prit part à la célèbre bataille de Sidi Rezegh le 21 Novembre 1941, qui valut au Lt. Ward Gunn une Victoria Cross posthume. L'emblème de division se trouve au-dessus de l'insigne régimental—qui est le numéro '55' peint en blanc sur fond bleu et rouge, code de la Royal Artillery.

E (en haut) Le taureau noir est l'insigne de la 11th Armoured Division; les insignes régimentaux du régiment intégral anti-char d'une division blindée étaient le numéro blanc '77' sur le fond bleu et rouge, couleurs de l'artillerie. **(en bas)** Le navire Viking est l'emblème de V Corps, et la plaque bleue et rouge de l'artillerie est surmontée de la barre blanche de tout régiment sous le commandement des Corps. Les pelles à l'arrière du M10 sont pour l'infanterie d'escorte.

F1 Tenue de corvée du désert type, avec manteau court, et le 'ceinturon de corvée' aux couleurs du régiment. **F2** La combinaison réglementaire gris/vert pâle des troupes blindées US portée avec la version d'Eté du *overseas cap* (le calot). Ce calot est bordé de jaune, de bleu et de rouge, désignant les trois branches de l'armée ayant fourni les effectifs de la Tank Destroyer Force—cavalerie, artillerie et infanterie. La bordure officielle noire et orange fut autorisée en Mars 1943. **F3** La tenue de corvée type du soldat US dans le Pacifique est accompagnée du casque de l'équipage de char. **G4** Le béret khaki remplaça le calot en 1943. Ce commandant d'un canon auto-moteur porte à l'épaule les insignes suivants: (de haut en bas) 30 Corps; la Royal Artillery; et le grade de sergent d'artillerie. Le casque sans bordure était celui de l'équipage de véhicules blindés. **G5** Bonnet original des marins francais, et insignes francais, accompagné d'un uniforme fourni par les Américains. **G6** Cet officier porte le blouson réglementaire des équipages de chars d'assaut; le pantalon imperméable de l'infanterie; et des bottes faites à partir de bottes d'officier de l'avantguerre. Le casque porte le motif d'épaule des Tank Destroyer Forces, que l'on remarque aussi sur la manche gauche; au-dessous, l'insigne indiquant le grade de l'officier. Sur le côté du casque, un autre motif reproduisant le drapeau du groupe; et à l'arrière, une barre verticale blanche indique qu'il est officier.

H (en haut) En Italie, cette couleur, dont le nom officiel était 'boue claire', était parfois adoptée par l'armée britannique pour ses véhicules, ordinairement peints d'un vert olive. Ce véhicule n'a que son numéro d'immatriculation et son nom, 'Defiant'. **(en bas)** Le numéro '46' sur plaque bleue et rouge est l'insigne du régiment intégral anti-chars d'une division d'infanterie. La plaque centrale indique la batterie et la troupe; la plaque de droite est celle de la 15th Division.

Farbtafeln

A Der Kanonier (links) gibt den Befehl zum Schiessen; sein Assisten (rechts) bereitet sich vor die Schnur zu ziehen, um das Geschütz abzufeuern, während der Lader sich aus dem Wege des zurücklaufenden Verschlussstückes hinlegt. Drei Reihen 'Munitionsaufbewahrröhre' sind sichtbar, wovon zwei sich in einer 'Bühne' unter den Deckplatten befinden. Unten kann man die allgemeine Inneneinrichtung des Fahrzeugs, mit dunkel angedeuteter 'Bühne' sehen.

B (oben) Von Zeit zu Zeit waren die US Panzerfahrzeuge nicht durchaus *Olive Drab* angestrichen, sondern grob mit einer helleren Farbe getarnt—gewöhnlicherweise in Sizilien oder Italien, wie hier der Fall ist. Die wiederholten weissen Sterne auf diesm M10 deuten auf eine Ängstlichkeit, dass die Mannschaften an den Händen voreiliger freundlicher Artilleristen leiden könnten! **(unten)** Typischer einfacher *Olive Drab* Anstrich, dessen einzige Aussergewöhnlichkeit in der Tatsache liegt, dass die Fahrzeuge der Vordertruppen selten die volle Reihe der Bezeichnungen trugen, wodurch die Einheit erkennbar war. Diese Markierungen bedeuten: '3A' = US 3rd Army; '705TD' = das Bataillon: 'B-14' = die Kompagnie und das einzelne Fahrzeug.

C (oben) Die berühmten 'Fusiliers Marins' haben die Namen ihrer ehemaligen Schiffe auf ihre M10 angestrichen. Das 'Y' bedeutet das Regiment innerhalb der Division, die drei senkrechten Stäbe, die Kompagnie: die Lage der Kompagniesmarkierung, den Zug; die Landkarte Frankreichs mit darübergelegtem Lothringerkreuz ist das Divisionsemblem. **(unten)** Der Titel 'Don't Want 'A' (hab) keine Lust) und das im Badeanzug gekleidete Pin-up-Girl sind zusätzliche Markierungen nach Wunsch der Mannschaft. Das '16' bedeutet eine Gewichtsklassierung in Beziehung auf die Tragfähigkeit der Brücken.

D Fahrzeug des Regiments, das zu Sidi Rezegh am 21. November 1941 die berühmte Aktion bekämpfte, worin der Leutnant Ward Gunn ein postumes VC verdiente. Das Divisionsemblem liegt oberhalb des Regimentskennzeichen, das weisse Schlüsselnummer '55' auf der rot-blauen Grundfarbe der Royal Artillery.

E (oben) Der schwarze Stier ist das Divisionsemblem der 11th Armoured Division; zu dieser Zeit war die weisse Nummer '77' das Kennzeichen des integrierten Panzerabwehrregiments einer Panzerdivision, auf der rotblauen Grundfarbe der Artillerie übergelegt wurde. **(unten)** Der Wikingschiff ist das Emblem des V Corps, und das rot-blaue Kennzeichen der Artillerie trägt oben den weissen Stab mit der Bedeutung eines Regiments, das vom Korps befehligt war. Die Spaten hinten am M10 sind für die mitfahrende Infanterie.

F1 Typische unzeremonielle Uniform des Wüstensoldats, mit kurzabgeschnittenem Wintermantel und 'Stallgurt' in den Regimentsfarben. **F2** Die vorschriftsmässige hellgrau-grüne einteilige Combinuform der US Panzertruppen und Fahrzeugsschlosser, mit der Sommerfeldmütze—*overseas cap* getragen. Die Mütze ist mit gelbem, rotem and blauem Schnurbesatz versehen, die Farben der drei Waffengattungen aus denen die Mannschaften für die Tank Destroyer Force (Panzerzerstörerformation) herstammten: Kavallerie, Artillerie und Infanterie. Ab März 1943 wurde einen amtlichen schwarz-orangen Schnurbesatz genehmigt. **F3** Der typische zweiteilige Feldanzug der US Soldaten im Stillen Ozean wird mit dem Sturzhelm der Panzermannschaften getragen. **G4** Die Feldmütze wurde im Jahre 1943 durch die khaki-Baskenmütze ersetzt. Dieser Kommandeur eines Geschützes auf selbstfahrender Lafette trägt folgende Kennzeichen am Ärmel: von oben nach unten: 30 Corps; Royal Artillery; Rangzeichen eines Artillerie-sergeants. Der Stahlhelm ohne Ränder wurde von den Mannschaften der Panzerfahrzeuge getragen. **G5** Original französische Matrosenmütze mit amerikanischer Ausgabeuniform getragen. **G6** Dieser Offizier trägt eine Windjacke, wie den Panzermannschaften ausgegeben wurde; wetterdichte Panzerinfanteriehosen; und Stiefel aus kurzgeschnittenen vorkriegs-Offiziersstiefel hergestellt. Vorne am Helm trägt er ein Abzug des Tuchabzeichens der Tank Destroyer Force, das auch an seinem linken Ärmel zu sehen ist; unter dem befindet sich sein Rangabzeichen. An der Seite des Helmes befindet sich ein zweiter Abzug in Form der Fahne seiner Gruppe und hinten ein weisser Stab, der ihn als Offizier bezeichnet.

H (oben) In Italien wurde diese Farbe, amtlich als *light mud* (hell-Dreck) bezeichnet, manchmal auf britischen Fahrzeugen anstatt dem gewöhnlichen Olivengrün gebraucht. Die einzige Kennzeichen dieses Fahrzeugs sind die Seriennummer und sein Name—'Defiant'. **(unten)** Die Nummer '46' auf rotblauem Grund ist das Kennzeichen des integrierten Panzerabwehrregiments einer Infanteriedivision. In der Mitte befindet sich das Kennzeichen der Batterie und des Trupps; rechts das Kennzeichen der 15th Division.